DATE DUE

SEP 2 3 1966		
Sharp		
APR 22 '68		
APR 29 '69		
NOV 5 5 71		
AP 15 '85		
TRACY		
GAYLORD		PRINTED IN U.S.A.

About the Book

This is the story of a people who have changed the way they live without changing themselves. The reason for the new way of life is the division of their country into two parts, Communist North Korea and free South Korea. The southern section, once agricultural, has had to learn to make the industrial products it once bought from the North. The northern section, once industrial, has had to raise the food it once bought from the South.

For many centuries other countries have fought their wars on Korea's soil. Hence the ancient Korean saying: "When the whales fight, the shrimps get hurt." Yet in spite of this troubled history and in spite of the splitting of the country after World War II, the families we visit in this book know how to make the most of life in the present. We share the excitement of an archery contest in a rice paddy, watch sorceress and sword dances performed to the music of hourglass drums and a zither played with a bow, propel a sled over a frozen river by means of pointed sticks and learn how to make a seesaw from a board and a rolled-up straw bag.

We make such good friends with our hosts that when we leave them we share their hope for the day when "the shrimps in the sea" are free to swim as they choose.

About the Author

As a boy, RICHARD JOHNSTON hoped to become, in order of preference, a farmer, prizefighter or band leader. A stint on the staff of the University of Alabama student newspaper changed his ambitions and his first job was as a copy boy on *The New York Times*. He became war correspondent in Europe and Korea for that paper and subsequently their foreign correspondent in the Far East, spending six years in Korea. He has received nine awards from the *Times* for outstanding reporting.

About the Illustrator

CLAUDINE NANKIVEL grew up in an artists' colony in Englewood, New Jersey; then studied at the Art Students League in New York, as well as in Paris and Fontainebleau. This is the sixth *Getting to Know* book she has illustrated.

About the *Getting to Know* Series

This series not only covers everyday life in many countries and regions and includes their geography and history — it also highlights *what's new today*. The series offers timely — and often first — reports on the birth of new nations in Africa and Asia, the splitting of ancient nations like China, the let's-get-together movement of members of Europe's and Latin America's Common Markets, and the struggle of two thirds of the world to attain the good life possessed by the other third. *To keep each book up to date in these fast-changing times, it is revised with every new printing.*

Specific countries in the *Getting to Know* series are determined by a survey of curriculum specialists in the fifty states. Made every two years, the survey is used to relate GTK subject matter to classroom needs. To insure intimacy as well as immediacy, authors are chosen first of all for the quality of their personal experience with the subject matter. All *Getting to Knows* are also checked by experts prior to publication.

Getting to Know
THE TWO KOREAS

by RICHARD J. H. JOHNSTON

Illustrated by CLAUDINE NANKIVEL

COWARD-McCANN, Inc.   NEW YORK

To my patient wife
Betty

I am indebted for the historical background of this book to the late Homer Bezaleel Hulbert, who spent a great part of his life in Korea and who saw The Hermit Kingdom arouse from a sleep of a thousand years. He died in Seoul in 1949, having written the first thorough account of Korea and its people to be published by a foreigner. Some years later, Alleyne Ireland made another contribution to our understanding of the Land of the Morning Calm by telling the story of Korea under the Japanese in a book, published in 1926, called *The New Korea*. Just as Dr. Hulbert's *History of Korea* traced the story of the country and its people from the dim past to the twentieth century, *The New Korea* tells of its life after nearly two decades under the conqueror's boot. The old history of Korea ended in September 1945, when its southern half was liberated from Japan by the United States and its northern half was occupied by the Soviet Union. Since that time Korea's history has been tragic and turbulent. It was the privilege of the author of this book to be in Korea for *The New York Times* during the perilous and exciting periods that followed.

Library of Congress Catalog Card Number: 65-10885

Editor of this series: Sabra Holbrook

MANUFACTURED IN THE UNITED STATES OF AMERICA
082012

SOVIET
MANCHURIA
TUMEN RIVER
DIAMOND MTS.
NORTH KOREA
SEA OF
YALU RIVER
TAEDONG R.
CHINA
SUNCHON
PYONGYANG
38TH PARALLEL
KOREA BAY
PANMUNJOM
SEOUL
KIMPO
HAN R.
INCHON
SOUTH KOREA
NAKTONG R.
YELLOW SEA
CHINA
JAPAN
KOREA STRAIT
CHEJU-DO
QUELPART IS.
EAST CHINA SEA
TAIWAN
HONGKONG
SOUTH CHINA SEA

If you were an astronaut flying high over the Pacific Ocean near Japan and looked down to earth you would see a peninsula stretching south from the northeast coast of Asia that would remind you of a crouching rabbit. The rabbit's long, pointed ears touch the easternmost part of the Soviet Union and its nose and forehead snuggle against China. Its paws and stomach dip into the Yellow Sea. Its folded hind legs rest on the Korean Strait and its back is turned to the Sea of Japan.

This rabbit-shaped piece of the world is Korea. The Korean peninsula, 600 miles long and 135 miles wide, is about the size of the state of Michigan. Its northern boundaries are marked by two rivers, the Yalu River which separates Korea from China, and the Tumen which is the border with the Soviet Union. The steep cliffs of the east coast rise straight up from the sea, while the southern and western shorelines are broken up by hundreds of islands and inlets.

Although the peninsula lies on the other side of the world from the United States, it is less than twenty-four hours away from our west coast by jet plane and what happens there can affect us deeply and immediately. Sixty-four thousand American soldiers have died in Korea. Later in this book you will find out why.

Korean soil has been a battleground for centuries. A little less than four hundred years ago, in 1592, just one hundred years after Columbus discovered the New World, a Japanese warlord, Hideyoshi, decided he would conquer the world, starting with Korea. He sent a huge army with cannons and firebombs, which were weapons the Koreans had never seen. At first the Japanese overran much of the country. Then one of Korea's greatest heroes, Admiral Yi Sun Sin, invented a new kind of warship, the "Turtle Boat," said to be the first ironclad warship the world has ever known. With this craft, he burned and sank the wooden ships of the Japanese. This victory gave the Korean people so much encouragement that they threw the Japanese out of their country with the help of Chinese soldiers.

For a long time afterward China and Korea thought of themselves as Big Brother and Little Brother. Every year the Korean king sent gifts to China's ruler to show his appreciation of their help. Some writers of history say that Korea was just a slave to China in the old days. It's true that China was the master, but it's also true that for nearly three hundred years Korea benefited from Chinese protection. The country was left to itself and the people developed the special arts which still flourish today: painting and poetry and the making of fine porcelains, pottery and brass work. Korean scholars wrote histories and recorded the lives of the Korean kings. Scholars were highly honored by the kings and greatly respected by the people. Writers put down tales of magic and wrote fables to explain nature. During that long period the Koreans had so little contact with the rest of the world that outsiders gave it the name of "Hermit Kingdom." Koreans, however, preferred to call their country The Land of the Morning Calm.

At the close of the nineteenth century, this calm time came to an end. Other nations suspected that there was gold and silver in Korea. They were also interested in the country as a gateway to the rest of the Asian continent. Most interested of all were the Japanese, Korea's neighbors across the sea to the east. They had become jealous of China's rule over the Koreans and decided to end it. They declared war on China. China was weak at the time and the Japanese got a foothold in Korea. They kept pushing farther into the country. By 1910 Korea was a Japanese colony. Koreans were declared to be subjects of the Emperor of Japan.

The Japanese rule was extremely harsh. It affected every aspect of the people's lives. They were even forbidden to study or write or speak their own language. Nevertheless the Koreans had no choice but to bow to it.

JAPANESE
INVASION

In 1919, the Koreans tried to tell the world about their sufferings by staging a peaceful demonstration for freedom. The Japanese put down this demonstration by killing and jailing thousands of unarmed Koreans. Few people outside the country knew what was really happening. The Japanese told the rest of the world that the Koreans had to be dealt with forcefully because they were primitive and dangerous and unable to govern themselves.

The Japanese rule continued until Japan was defeated in World War II. After the war Korea was occupied by United States troops on the southern side of the 38th parallel, and by Soviet troops on the northern side. The parallel divides the country exactly in half. Korea has remained divided at that line ever since.

GENERAL
MACARTHUR

In 1950, the government established by the Soviets in the north sent troops to invade the south. The United Nations went to the aid of South Korea. It was at this time that American soldiers fought and died on Korean soil — along with other U.N. troops. An American General, Douglas MacArthur, was named Commander of the U.N. forces which finally stopped the invaders.

We speak today of two Koreas, the Communist North and the independent South, but we cannot speak of two different kinds of Korean people. One day the 30,000,000 Koreans hope to be re-united under one government at peace with the world, with no foreigners interfering in their affairs. There is an ancient Korean saying — "When the whales fight the shrimps get hurt." By this the Koreans mean that little countries like their own suffer when big countries go to war.

The Koreans' history goes back a long, long time. The first known people to come to the peninsula were Mongolian tribesmen who may have been looking for better land for crops and better places to graze cattle. A number of these people are believed to have moved on to the east, possibly crossing the Bering Strait into North America to become the ancestors of some of our Indian tribes. There is a curious likeness between the art of certain American Indians and art handed down through the ages in Korea. The thunderbird pattern is one of these likenesses. The copper-colored skin of Koreans also is somewhat like the Indian complexion.

As in other lands where history is so old that facts have been forgotten, the Koreans invented myths about where they came from and who they are. One of the most ancient of these myths is the story of Tan Gun. This mythical ancestor is said to have sprung magically from the sky. He married a woman who sprang mysteriously from the ground. They had two sons who also married women that rose from the earth — and so the Korean people were supposed to have begun.

Although Koreans are Oriental, with a few exceptions their looks and habits differ from those of their Oriental neighbors. They are fairer-skinned than the Japanese, not as yellow-complexioned as the Chinese and taller than both of these neighbors. Only the almond-shaped eyes are the same. The Koreans are fond of jokes and like to poke fun and laugh at themselves. The Japanese, a more serious people, find this humor hard to understand. The Koreans are more like the Chinese in their habit of making merry and laughing aloud.

The Korean language, written in ideographs, or symbols that stand for ideas, is meaningless to a Chinese or a Japanese. When Korean writers make up poems or special compositions, they write with brushes and they take as much care with their brush strokes as with the thoughts they wish to express. This art of painting ideas is called calligraphy.

In addition to ideographs, Koreans have an alphabet of twenty-four letters which everybody knows, and since there are no dialects in the Korean language, people from all over the country have no difficulty understanding each other. In many Asian countries dialects differ so much that they are almost like different languages.

There are three forms of Korean speech however, which every child learns in school. The forms are low, middle and high. The high form is proper for addressing elders and other respected people. The middle form is for everyday use. The low form is spoken to children — with one exception. It is never used by a woman or girl addressing a boy. Females use the middle form when talking with males in the family. With other men, they use the high form.

Although the people of North and South Korea speak and think alike, the land makes their living conditions quite different. In the north, near the eastern coast, are the towering Diamond Mountains, over 9,000 feet high. Deer, wolves and foxes roam in the

FOX

WOLF   DEER

mountains, beavers make homes in the streams and squirrels and
owls live in the trees. The land is dry, rugged and hard to farm,
but the people do manage to grow some wheat and barley. To the
south the mountain peaks flatten out and the broad and fertile
land between them is lush with graceful willows, roses, violets and
daffodils. And most important of all, here is the great rice-growing
region of the country, well irrigated by rivers.

The most important rivers in Korea run from the north toward the southwest. They are the Yalu and Taedong in the north, the Han in the center and the Naktong in the south. Many of the rivers can carry small boats or junks, square-shaped vessels, nearly a hundred miles inland from the sea.

In early summer, which is the rainy season, the rivers swell, and even dry gullies become torrents. As the water sweeps to the sea, it carries precious soil with it. In this season southern farmers toil day and night without sleeping to try to keep the floods from washing away their rice paddies. In a single day a farmer's rice crop for the entire year can be destroyed. Bridges, houses, sometimes whole villages go, too.

The main reason for these terrible washouts is the lack of forests in the north. Over centuries, many pines, spruces, elms and oaks

have been chopped down. Especially during World War II, the Japanese stripped away the trees for the lumber. Now the bare hillsides and mountainsides can't hold back the water which rushes southward through the country. Efforts to repair the damage by planting new trees have made little progress because so many people go out at night and chop down the newly planted trees for firewood.

Besides washing out farms and villages, the floods also wash out what roads there are. In fact, it is only recently that roads have been built capable of taking cars and trucks. Even these are just single-track graveled lanes that wander through the mountains or follow along the edges of the rice paddies, leading from village to village.

You can see that travel in Korea isn't easy. There are only two major railroad lines in the two Koreas. One runs north and south in North Korea; the other runs north and south in South Korea. Some smaller lines connect Seoul, the capital of South Korea, with Inchon, the port for Seoul, and with one point on the east coast.

There is a big airport at Kimpo, not far from Seoul, where planes land from the United States, the Philippines, Japan and Hong Kong. The North Koreans have a similar airport near their capital, Pyongyang, where planes come and go from China and the Soviet Union. There is no railroad, no airline, no travel of any kind between the two Koreas. Relatives living on either side of the dividing line have almost no way to keep in touch with each other because their governments are enemies.

The North Korean government is something like that of the Soviet Union. North Koreans vote for candidates named by the Communist Party. It is the only political party and there is only one candidate for every position. The parliament elected in this way is called a *presidium*. The top government official, who is also the leader of the Communist party, is the prime minister.

South Korea has several political parties and a National Assembly elected by the people. The Assembly elects a prime minister who chooses a president. In recent years, however, the army has controlled the government, with generals serving as prime ministers or premiers. Several times South Korean governments, both military and non-military have been ousted because the people were dissatisfied. One of the biggest objections of the people was the extent to which officials used their government positions to make money for themselves instead of to serve the people. Young students, who objected most, were the leaders of these revolts. Although the South Korean government is not a Communist dictatorship like that in the north, it isn't a government that you would consider entirely free, nor does it satisfy the Korean people.

After the country was divided, the people in both parts had to learn to do things they had never done before. South Korea had to build power plants to produce electricity that used to come from the north. They had to build factories to make the cloth and cement and other necessities that were once made in the north and they had to begin to buy things from other countries — like coal and iron — that used to be supplied by the north. North Korea had to

find ways to raise food to replace the supply that no longer came from the south. Korean life was changed more in a few years than it had been in centuries. Yet all these changes didn't change the Korean people themselves.

On solemn occasions Koreans are very dignified, but they also love good times. They are great talkers and storytellers and they love music and dancing. You would find them delightful hosts, for they make friends quickly with strangers. However, they never pretend they like people just for the sake of being polite.

Most Koreans are Buddhists. Buddhists believe that men achieve joy through good thoughts and deeds and by forgetting about material wants. They believe that the greatest joy is to be found in Nirvana, the Buddhist heaven, but it is expected that men will have to live several lives before they can reach it. Many devout male Buddhists become monks who live chiefly in remote places in the mountains. They come down to beg for food and are a common sight in South Korean towns and cities as they go about in their yellow robes, carrying brass begging bowls.

In North Korea the government is trying to stamp out Buddhism. It wants Communism to take the place of any religion. The government has also driven out Christian missionaries.

Toward the end of the nineteenth century Christian missionaries went to Korea in great numbers. They converted many Koreans and gained the affection of many more through kindly work. They built not only churches but much-needed schools and hospitals.

In addition to their faith in Christianity or Buddhism, many Korean people, particularly those in the country, cling to belief in spirits. Some spirits are thought to be good and helpful. The people make offerings of food and trinkets at certain times of the year. For instance, when rice is planted in the spring, spirits are offered food and asked to help bring in a good crop. Evil spirits are chased away by noises and dances. The eaves of Korean houses curl upward so that any evil spirits who land on top of the house will be bounced far out of the yard when they slide down the roof.

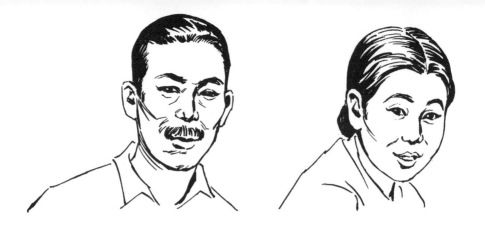

The best way to get to know Koreans is to visit a family. Suppose you are invited to spend a holiday with one of Korea's many Kim families. Their name is as common there as Jones or Smith is in our country. Kim Sung Kee, the father, is a farmer who lives ten miles west of Seoul. In the old fashioned way, the Kim family still keeps the family name first. More westernized Koreans sometimes turn the name around so that the family name is last, like ours. This saves foreigners from making embarrassing mistakes such as calling Kim Sung Kee, "Mr. Kee," when he is really Mr. Kim.

Mr. Kim has four acres of rice land, a couple of peach trees, an apple tree, persimmon trees and a tiny garden patch for pumpkins, watermelons, sweet potatoes, radishes, squash and peppers. When the peppers are ripe, they will be spread on straw mats to dry in the sun. Then they are ground on a stone to make a hot, spicy powder which you will taste in some of your food while visiting the Kims.

Mr. Kim works his land with plow and hoe and he has an ox to help him. His three-room house is made of sticky red mud smeared on a lattice work of twigs. Over part of the straw roof a tangle of squash and pumpkin vines are growing.

Mr. Kim's wife is Kim Eun Hee. They have a ten-year-old boy, Kim Chun Won, and an eight-year-old girl, Kim Yun Sook.

It's early in the morning when you arrive, but Mr. Kim has already eaten and gone to a small shed behind his house to feed grass and rice husks to his ox. Mrs. Kim is also out back of the house in a roofed-over space where she is cooking the children's breakfast on an open charcoal fire. She has rice bubbling in an iron pot. The children have risen from their beds on the floor, folded the bed covers carefully and put them into a small cupboard.

The stone floor of the house, covered with layers of varnished paper, is cool for sleeping even when the weather is warm. In the winter it is heated by a small firepot under the house. Opposite the firepot, also under the house, is the base of a small chimney. The entire space is sealed in. When the pot is lighted, the hot air circulates, warming the stone floor above. The smoke escapes through the chimney. This kind of heating has been used for thousands of years in Korea. Only recently in western countries have architects learned to use the same principle in the steam and electric heated floors of super-modern homes and buildings.

Before breakfast Kim Chun Won washes his face and hands and puts on short trousers and a black jacket which buttons up to his throat. He slips on his little rubber shoes. His sister wears a pleated blue skirt, a blue blouse, a scarf and rubber shoes. Chun Won's books are in a canvas knapsack that he will carry on his back. His sister's books are tied in a scarf.

For breakfast you have rice, a small piece of meat and a few pieces of *kim chi,* which is a spicy side dish of pickled cabbage, garlic and red pepper. You and the children each have a tiny cup of tea to finish off the meal. You need the tea after the kim chi. It's very hot on the tongue and has such a powerful odor that it's kept outside the house in earthenware jars. Koreans think it is a substitute for sunshine in the winter and helps keep their teeth strong and white. Maybe they are right.

If you were visiting the Kims during the fall, you might also have sweet, ripe persimmons after breakfast. In fact, you would be biting happily into them all day long. Chun Won and Yun Sook have already begun to watch their persimmon trees hopefully, even though it will be several months before frost turns the green fruit to brilliant red and the soft orange insides are ready to eat.

Before breakfast, Mrs. Kim has put on the white wrap-around dress and the rubber shoes with turned-up toes which she will wear for the day. Her hair is done up tight to her head with a bun in the back. Before she was married she wore her hair down, but like a proper married woman, she now keeps her hairdress as plain as possible.

When Mr. Kim comes back from the shed you notice that he is dressed in loose fitting, white trousers, tied around his waist with

a piece of cord. His short-sleeved jacket is a dull brown. He's barefooted and will work that way all day.

The dishes are quickly washed and the children take you off to school, joining young friends on the road. The boys and girls walk separately. Occasionally, you pass a farmer's ox-cart. You walk the mile to school much faster than the cart could carry you.

In the one-story wooden school, the boys and girls study separately. Their subjects are Korean language and history, arithmetic and hygiene. Girls also learn sewing and home economics.

After six years in this school, the children can go on to three years of middle school and three years of high school where they will study more advanced subjects. Some of them may then attend one of the twenty-five free colleges which the government runs, or one of the mission colleges which charges a small fee.

Both Chun Won and Yun Sook learn from their teachers how important it is for the country to restore its forest lands, not only to prevent floods but to make homes for birds and animals. The wildlife of the country has decreased as the forests have disappeared. Even the great Siberian tigers which once roamed in the northern mountains are very scarce. In the last twenty-five years only one of these beasts has been seen.

Studies stop at lunch time while everybody eats a little cold rice, brought from home. Classes are also interrupted for morning and afternoon recesses, during which girls and boys play separately. Girls jump rope, or jump up and down on a teeter-totter board laid across one of the rolled-up straw bags used for packing rice. The girls take turns jumping down hard on one end of the board to throw the girl at the other end high in the air. Korean children have few toys from stores, so they use things around them to make up most of their own games.

Girls, incidentally, never play with dolls. Instead, they take care of real babies — their younger brothers and sisters. As soon as girls are seven or eight years old, they take turns minding younger members of the family whom they carry about on their backs in slings made from blankets. Sitting comfortably in the sling, babies go nearly everywhere with their sisters. Boys don't carry their smaller sisters or brothers. That's considered a girl's job.

Boys roll hoops or play with tops or toss stones in the air and catch them on the backs of their hands in a game something like jackstones. Stone and rock games have been handed down from a time when rock throwing was a serious business. Centuries ago the Japanese took all spears, swords and bows and arrows away from the Koreans. The Koreans fought the Japanese by throwing rocks and they became expert at this kind of warfare.

Recesses are too short for all the games Korean boys enjoy. After school, or during summer vacation, they play baseball, which they learned from the American soldiers stationed in their country. In the winter, when the breezes blow briskly along the river banks and in the open fields, they fly kites shaped like dragons and fish. The skies are dotted with the high-flying figures as the boys try to outdo each other in diving and swooping their kites in great circles. Both boys and girls like to speed across icebound rivers on little sleds with metal runners. They push themselves along by jabbing two pointed sticks into the ice. They also like to ice skate.

When the spring comes, girls have swinging contests to see who can swing highest and most gracefully. They make their own swings of straw-rope and hang them from the limbs of high trees.

While you are visiting school, Mr. Kim and his wife and neighbors have gone to the rice paddy. Kim has prepared the paddy by plowing the mud under the water. For many days his slow, patient ox has drawn a wooden plow back and forth, churning up the mud to make it soft for the plantings. Now Mr. Kim stretches string in straight rows where he wants the rice planted. The women pass along bundles of shoots which are pressed into the mud under the water. The planting has been going on for several days. This is the last day and the hard work will be over by the time you and the children return from school. It will be a night for rejoicing.

On this night the Kim family will have a feast. Mrs. Kim has already selected a plump chicken for the supper meal. She has brought out small packages of nuts and fruit for dessert. Koreans never eat any kind of cooked desserts.

Mr. Kim will eat alone and you and Mrs. Kim and the children must wait for your supper until he has finished. Koreans think that fathers, as the hardest workers of the family, are entitled to be left alone to eat in peace without a lot of chatter.

After supper Mr. Kim's neighbors gather in his front yard behind the high, mud wall that protects it from animals and intruders. The older men tell stories, the children romp and the women gossip about clothing and food. They also try to guess which unmarried girl in the neighborhood will be the next to have a young man ask her father for her hand.

A few of the older men may start an archery tournament. They are extremely good shots with bow and arrow. Some can hit a target no bigger than a man's hand from a hundred yards away. Kim Chun Won tells you that the best time to see a really big archery contest is on one of the two great national holidays. One is Samil Day, March 1st, when Koreans remember the brave but hopeless revolt of their forefathers against Japanese rule. The other is August 15th when they celebrate the victory over the Japanese and the establishment of their own government. Some of the stories the men tell at Mr. Kim's planting feast may be about these events in Korean history.

When darkness comes the children do some homework by the light of a candle while Mrs. Kim puts the house in order for the night. Mr. Kim and his men neighbors go off to thatched huts set on little raised platforms at the edges of the rice paddy. There they take turns watching through the night to see that no breaks occur in the dikes that might let precious water flow away from the fields. The dikes are made of mud, packed two or three feet high. The watchers also keep a sharp eye out to make sure that no thief steals the young plants. The Kim family's life depends on the rice crop. They will not only use it for food themselves, but will also sell it in order to buy what they need. They even pay some of their taxes with rice.

It will be difficult for the children to get to sleep this night, because they are so excited about tomorrow when the family is going to Seoul for a carnival that also celebrates the end of the spring planting. Mr. Kim has promised that they will see all the sights in the capital. Everyone will wear his best clothing for the outing.

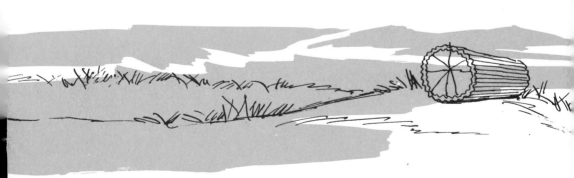

As you settle down for sleep, you hear frogs chirping merrily in the night and once in a while the bark of a dog. Chun Won whispers, "Let's sneak out in the courtyard." And you do. The stars glitter overhead with a million twinkling lights and Yun Sook remembers the wonderful story of the night sky of winter.

Many years ago a prince fell in love with a farmer's daughter, but he wasn't allowed to marry her because she was not of royal blood. The couple became sadder and sadder. Finally they died of grief. Good spirits learned about their sorrow and they told the white cranes to form a bridge high in the sky so that the prince might come from his royal heaven and the girl might leave her common people's heaven to meet in the sky for a little while. The cranes waited until the first cold weather came when they would no longer be busy caring for the little cranes that were hatched in the spring. Then one night they flew up into the sky by the millions and formed a bridge between the two heavens. They flapped their wings slowly, staying close together. The prince and the girl walked across the cranes' backs and met in the middle of the sky. As they walked, feathers began to fall from the cranes' backs. This was the first snow of winter. Anyone who doesn't believe this story must go to Korea. Early in the winter, if he looks up into the sky on a clear night, he will see the great bridge of cranes. We call it the Milky Way.

The next morning the Kim family rushes through breakfast. Mrs. Kim is wearing her prettiest wrap-around dress with a tight bodice and a silver hair pin pushed through the knot on the back of her head. The children have on their gayest holiday costumes. Kim Chun Won wears freshly-laundered, white, baggy trousers, tied at the ankles. His orange shirt has long, loose sleeves. His vest is bright blue with silver buttons. His hair is freshly trimmed and his white rubber shoes have been scrubbed.

His sister wears a wrap-around skirt like her mother's and a bodice of many colors. Her hair is bobbed. When she is ready for high school it will be allowed to grow long and will be braided and tied with a gay ribbon. She will keep that style until she gets married.

The walk to Seoul is long and the day is warm. More and more country people join the Kim family on the road. Many old friends call greetings, shouting *"Aniya simnika,"* which means, "Hello. How are you?"

"Cho sumnida," replies Mr. Kim. He is saying, "Very fine."

As you approach Seoul through the East Gate, you hear the booming sound of the Great Bell on Chong-no Square.

Reaching the square, you see that a dozen men are pulling on the ropes of a tremendous log attached to a tripod beside the bell. Mr. Kim tells you that the men pulling the ropes are very important people. It is considered a great honor to take part in the ringing. The men use the log like a battering ram to strike the great bell, ten feet tall and nearly six feet wide, that hangs from a scaffolding.

Once the bell hung in a great temple. The temple burned but the people rescued the bell. It was precious to them, for it had a long tradition in Korean history. When the Japanese occupied Korea they forbade the people to ring the bell, but rebels managed to ring it once anyway — at the time of their revolt against the Japanese. After that it was silent for a quarter of a century — until it bonged forth on the day American soldiers arrived at Seoul, September 7, 1945.

As you approach the booming bell Mr. Kim tells you its tale. Several hundred years ago when the Great Bell was to be cast in

honor of a king, wise men gathered to decide what should go into the melting of metals for it. They decided that this, the greatest of bells, should contain many precious things, including gold, silver and jewels. The king ordered everyone who could attend the casting of the bell to bring the thing most precious to him and add it to the melting metals.

People of wealth cast in their jewels and rings to impress the king. At last the riches in the mold cooled and the mold was removed. The handsome bell gleamed like no jewel ever seen. It was hoisted into place. The striking log was put up and the highest officials of the court tugged the log to let it strike the bell. At the first stroke it rang with a wonderful, deep roar. But when the log hit the bell a second time, the bell cracked. There was great confusion among the wise men because the bell was supposed to last forever.

The wise men held a meeting to consider what had gone wrong. They discussed the matter for days and finally went to the king with their decision. Someone, they said, had been present at the casting who had a precious thing but didn't throw it into the cauldron. This person must be found so that the bell might be recast properly.

The king sent out an order that everyone who had been present at the first casting must return for a second one, bringing with him his most precious possession.

As people began again to throw precious things into the melting pot the wise men saw a poor peasant woman on the edge of the crowd. On her back, riding in a blanket-sling, was a small baby. The wise men cried out that here was the precious thing that had not gone into the first casting. Before the king could stop them, the wise men tore the baby from its mother's back and hurled it into the cauldron.

The king tried to comfort the heartbroken mother by offering to grant her many wishes, but she had only one wish — to have her baby back. This the king could not grant.

When the metals cooled down, a day was set for the ringing. As the bell struck the second, third and even twentieth time the sound of a baby's cry was heard. *Emil le chong,* it said, Emil le chong. This is Korean for mother.

As the Kims near Chong-no square they hear the cry and so do you. The sound of the bell has a note exactly like a Korean infant's wail for his mother, and the story Mr. Kim has just told is the way Koreans explain it.

At Seoul Grounds, a great open arena, you find the carnival. There are jugglers and acrobats and dancers and magicians. Girls in fluttering full skirts ride on swings in a contest to see who can go highest. At the edge of the grounds boys fly their kites. Mr.

Kim buys rice candies from vendors for all of you. The candy is a great treat, for there is very little of it in Korea.

He pays for the candy in *won*. In recent years five won have equaled an American penny, but the value of the won changes from time to time, depending on how poor or how well-off the country is.

Even though the rice candy is delicious, you almost forget to munch it in the excitement of watching the acrobats. You catch your breath in wonder at the daring of a small boy balanced on top of a swaying bamboo pole that rests upright in a cup on his father's forehead.

HARVEST FESTIVAL

You could happily spend hours at the carnival, but the Kim family must leave in time to get home before dark. Before leaving they introduce you to city cousins, the Choi family, with whom you will spend the next few days.

The father, Choi Chung Ko is a motorman on a Seoul streetcar that runs from Yongdongpo, a suburb, to Ulchiro, a busy shopping street in the city. Mr. Choi provides very well for his family now, but he and his wife have been through hard days in the past. They were among the one million refugees who fled from the Communists in North Korea in the four and a half years after World War II. They lived for some time in a refugee camp in South Korea until Mr. Choi found a way to start life over.

The two children were born in the south and now the family lives in a red brick house with a green tile roof. The courtyard in front of the house is full of flowering shrubs taken care of by a yard boy who works for several families on the street.

The Choi home has steam heat and one room furnished in western style with two chairs, a sofa and a china closet. Mr. Choi has many western friends. He has been often in their homes and likes their way of living, so he decided to have one room like theirs. His other rooms are in Korean style. There are a few small chests, low tables and cushions on the bare floors. At night, mattresses and quilted blankets are unrolled on the floors for sleeping. In the morning, they are hung out to air, then rolled up again. Mr. Choi sleeps in the biggest room, which he has all to himself, as is the Korean custom for fathers.

But although the Chois follow customs such as this one, they have also adopted many western ways. Mr. Choi dresses in western style and so do his wife, Choi In Su, and his children. Do Yun, their son, is a student in the Seoul Central High School and their daughter, Im Hi, is in her last year in grammar school.

The Chois have several modern conveniences in their house. Mrs. Choi has a sewing machine and a refrigerator, and the family has a radio and television set. Since there's only one television station in Seoul, however, they don't have any choice of programs.

Some of the television shows are films given to Korea by the U.S. government. These are in English, which the Choi children speak very well. Both began to study it in grammer school. Mrs. Choi doesn't understand much English, but Mr. Choi who has talked to many Americans, gets along fairly well with the language.

The family goes to the movies at Seoul Theater once a week and Mr. Choi spends one or two evenings a week at a club where he plays Baduk — a kind of checkers game — with his friends. He has been saving money to buy a small, secondhand automobile. Now the family travels mostly by streetcar.

For dinner at the Chois' home, you have a special delicacy — whale steak. With her refrigerator Mrs. Choi is able to keep fresh fish. She is also able to buy it in the Seoul market. Mrs. Choi has a girl to help her with the marketing, cooking and housework. Chang Su Im, the daughter of a neighbor of the Kim family, wanted to come to the city, so she works for Mrs. Choi in return for her board and keep.

Su Im notices how much you enjoy the whale steak and promises that on other nights you will feast on squid, octopus, whitefish and bass. Su Im still finds fresh fish a great treat, for she had only dried fish before she came to the city. Although fish is plentiful along the coast, it is shipped only to the big cities because transportation elsewhere is too long and difficult.

When you have finished a big dinner, Su Im comes to offer you a platter of rice. You have already had rice with your meal and you couldn't possibly eat more. You are stuffed. This is fortunate, because you are not supposed to touch this rice. If you did, it would be an insult to the Chois — a sign that their meal hadn't been sufficient. It's offered to you to show that Mr. Choi can afford to serve more than is needed. But the rice won't go to waste — Su Im will eat it all. She watches you a little anxiously, hoping you understand you are not supposed to take any.

The rice came from the Kim family farm. Last year Mr. Choi took a day off from his job and went to help his cousin with the harvest. He tells you about it now.

SQUID

OCTOPUS

The rice stood tall and yellow, the tops filled to bursting with fat grain. It was a good crop and there was shouting and singing as the sickles swept through the stalks. The cut stalks were tied into great sheaves and carried to the front yard of the farmhouse. There the sheaves were opened and the grain spread on the hard earth. Flails made of two long sticks joined together were used to beat the rice grains from the tops of the stalks. The grains were tossed in front of a fan made by attaching four paddles to a tripod. A neighbor too old to do heavy work in the fields turned a crank that spun the paddles. The chaff blew away and the hard rice kernels fell onto straw mats. On a windy day, Mr. Kim wouldn't have bothered with the fan. The harvesters would have thrown the grain into the air and let the wind separate the chaff.

After cleaning, the kernels were scooped into straw bags and shipped to market. Mr. Kim kept enough to see his family through the winter and he gave Mr. Choi a *suk* of rice for helping with the harvest. The suk — about two bushels — saved the Choi family from having to spend money for expensive rice in the city markets.

After dinner the children tell you about their plans for the future. Choi Do Yun is studying to be an engineer and he wants to go to Seoul National University when he finishes high school.

His sister is studying the violin and expects to be a music teacher.

Many youngsters with musical talent have gone abroad in recent years to study western music. Several good Korean symphony orchestras perform the works of western composers. At the same time there is an important effort to preserve the country's own musical traditions. Music that sounds strange at first to a foreigner's ear, but very pleasant to Koreans, is played by the Royal Palace Orchestra in Seoul. The Chois take you to a performance the next evening. The instruments include cymbals, bells and xylophones made with stone keys instead of metal or wooden ones. There is also the *taegeum* (a small flute), *t'ang-juk* (a larger flute), *hyang-piri* (a bamboo oboe), the *aejeng* (a zither played with a bow) and the *changgo*. The changgo is an hourglass-shaped drum with skins stretched across each end. The drummer plays one end with a reed and the other with a short, heavy stick.

Another instrument in the orchestra is the *kayakum,* which resembles a harp. The musician puts it flat on the floor and sits cross-legged in front of it. Then he plucks its six strings with a stick in his right hand, at the same time pressing down on the strings with his left hand.

The music played on these various instruments is hundreds of years old. Much of it was written for the entertainment of kings and their courts and ancient dances are performed to it. There is *nong-ak,* a farmer's dance, *chung-aeng-jun-mu,* a court dance, *mudang-choom,* a sorceress's dance and *kum-mu,* a sword dance. The one you watch is kum-mu.

In this dance two men carry swords so heavy that it takes both hands to wield them. Each dancer tries either to chop his opponent's head off, or to chop his feet out from under him. The dancers you watch only pretend to chop of course, but long ago the chopping was real.

The day after this performance, the Chois take you to see the sights of Seoul. The original city is more than five hundred years old, but little of its past has survived except a few old palaces that now house museums and two of the four great archways that were once the entrances to the city. These entrances with their wooden gates were built into a forty-foot-high mud wall that guarded ancient Seoul. Still standing on top of the surviving archways are the tremendous pagoda-shaped barracks in which soldiers of emperors were once quartered. Their duty was to patrol the walls and watch out for invaders. The gates were closed at night, and up to the end of the nineteenth century, visitors who arrived after dusk had to ask special permission to enter the city. If the permission was granted, visitors were hauled up to the top of the wall, one by one, in a basket. The purpose was to prevent surprise attack by a group of people.

Modern Seoul has spread out beyond its old gates and today traffic circles have been built around them. The city is a hodge-podge of different kinds of buildings which tell the story of its

CITY GATE

fortunes. When the Japanese occupied Korea in 1910, they put up buildings in a style of architecture that was popular then. The president lives in one of these buildings today — a mansion which the Japanese made for their governor and which is called Kyung Mu Dai, or Place of Beautiful View. It overlooks Seoul from one of the four mountain peaks that surround the city. Koreans often call this mansion "The Blue House," because so much blue tile was used on the exterior.

The Blue House, the post office and a few other Japanese buildings survived the Korean War, during which eighty percent of Seoul was destroyed. When Americans came there after the war, they used rubble from the ruins to repair some of the buildings, and others they built new from chrome, glass and concrete. The new buildings are along Seoul's two main avenues, one running north and south, the other east and west. Back from these avenues, many people have their homes in little, high-walled alleys.

OLD PALACE

Some of the homes are new, like the Chois', but many are old-fashioned, shacklike dwellings. A wooden gate leads into the courtyard of each house. The houses have no numbers, so if you want to visit a friend, you must ask for him by name. The neighbors will be glad to tell you which house is his.

When you come back to the Chois' house after your trip around the city, there is a great excitement. The family has a conference in hushed tones. You try to be polite and not eavesdrop, but you can't help showing your curiosity. It is Do Yun who persuades his mother and father to tell you what is going on.

The Chois have received a message from uncle Park Huen Wook in North Korea. There is no mail between the two parts of the country, no telegraph or telephone, and a message from a rela-

38TH PARALLEL

tive is a very rare event. The means of bringing it are very dangerous.

North and South Korea are divided at the 38th parallel by a demilitarized and uninhabited zone five miles wide and 155 miles long. On the northern side of the zone are North Korean troops and their Soviet and Chinese advisers. On the southern side are the American and South Korean troops who make up the United Nations Command in Korea. If the opposing forces need to get in touch with each other, there are six contact points where they are permitted to confer. A principal one is Panmunjom, which Koreans sarcastically call "Peace Village." There is no village there, of course, and not much peace.

To cross this zone without being seen by the opposing troops who guard it is almost impossible. Therefore, the few who attempt to come south from North Korea take a very roundabout route. They go into Communist China, which is possible without much difficulty, then southward, where they join refugees from China who escape into the British colony of Hong Kong. From there they make their way to the island of Taiwan, which is, in effect, under American protection. Since Americans are also involved in South Korea, they are able to travel there from Taiwan. They travel about 1,500 miles to reach a country from which they are geographically separated by only five miles.

This is the route followed by smugglers and it is one of the smugglers who has brought the Chois the message from their uncle. He has also brought some jewelry which the Park family has managed to keep in hiding and which they would like to have the Chois exchange for clothes. The smuggler will bring the clothes back to the Parks.

The Parks live in Sunchon, a small village about fifty miles from Pyongyang. Mr. Park raises wheat, barley and oats and has a small apple orchard. He can keep about ten percent of these crops for himself. The rest he must sell to the government for whatever price the government chooses to pay him. Lately the government has been paying very little and that's why Mr. Park wants to trade the jewelry for clothes — especially for his twelve-year-old daughter Park In Hi and his ten-year-old son, Park Heun Chon.

Mr. Park's message doesn't say too much, because if the smuggler were caught with it, there would be trouble for the Parks. But the Chois, themselves refugees from the North, can read between the lines. They know what their uncle is talking about and they tell you about it, too.

They know that Park In Hi and Park Heun Chon are taught in school to report any action of their parents that seems critical of the government.

"Suppose," says Mr. Choi, "that uncle Heun Wook objects to going into a village to listen to a long speech about running dogs —"

"Running dogs?" you ask.

"Americans," Mr. Choi replies. "Koreans use the phrase running dogs the way you might say —" he hesitates for a word. You get the point. "Stinkers," you suggest. "Yes," Mr. Choi says, with a faint smile, "only maybe a little worse. So the Communists call Americans running dogs. Now this speech about the dogs is to be made just at the time uncle Heun Wook is ready to harvest his barley. Never mind, he has to go and he has to listen. The speech may be given by some official or it may be broadcast over the village radio. Either way, it will take hours and uncle Heun Wook wants to get home to his barley.

"Besides needing what grain he can keep for himself, he knows that he will be in trouble if he doesn't produce enough for the state. Time is precious.

"When our uncle finally gets home, he says that the meeting was a terrible waste of time. This is the kind of remark his children must report and for which he can be punished."

"But why would the children report it?" you ask.

"Probably they think it is right," Mr. Choi explains. "They were born after the Communists took over and they have been always to schools which teach them the Communist way. For instance, when

they study World War II, they are taught that the Soviet Union won the war all by itself. Nothing is said about the United States or England or France or other countries which, with the Soviets, formed the allied team that won. Why, even at recess time Heun Chon is learning how to use a gun. He's told he will need it to defend his village against attack by the running dogs and other imperialists. The Communists apply the word imperialist, which actually means a nation that owns and runs colonies for its own benefit, to any country which they consider an enemy.

"Besides," Mr. Choi goes on, "both Heun Chon and In Hi belong to the youth division of the Democratic People's Party, an organization which is not democratic at all. At its meetings they study the writings of Communist heroes and learn Communist doctrine. They also take part in parades on days that celebrate Communist victories and in demonstrations against people whom the Communists want them to hate.

"If the children's performance satisfies the leaders, they can go on to other organizations and eventually become members of the party itself. Then they will tell other people what to do instead of being told themselves."

Most of what Mr. Choi tells you is said quietly. But at one point, Mr. Choi becomes very emphatic. His voice rises. "None of this story," he says "has happened because Koreans wished it. We and uncle Heun Wook are not apart because we wanted to be."

You remember the old motto: "When the whales fight, the shrimps get hurt," and as the Chois go back to their discussion of what they can do about their uncle's request, you hope that some day the Parks and the Chois and all the people of the two Koreas may live in one country — in a world where whales have more important things to do than fight.

HOW TO PRONOUNCE FOREIGN WORDS *

Word	Pronunciation	Word	Pronunciation
Aniya simnika	*Ahn*-ee-ah *sim*-nee-kah	Naktong nong-ak	Nahk-tong *nong*-ahk
Baduk	Bah-*dook*	Panjmunjum	*Panj*-moon-joom
		Park Heun Chon	Park Hyoon Jon
changgo	*jung*-goh	Park Heun Wook	Park Hyoon Wuk
Chang Su Im	Jang-Soo-Eem	Park In Hi	Park Een Hee
Choi Chung Ko	Jeh Jung Koh	Pyongyang	*Pen*-yang
Chong-no	Jong-noh	pyungchang	pyung-jang
Cho sumnida	Jo soom-*nee*-dah		
chosun	*jo*-soon	samil	*sahm*-eel
chung-aeng-gun-mu	jung-ayeng-joon-moo	Seoul	Sole
		Sunchon	Soon-john
		suk	sook
Do Yun	Doh Yoon		
		Taedong	*Tah*-dong
Hideyoshi	*Hee*-dy'*oh*-shee	taegeum	*tah*-goom
hyang-piri	hyang-peer-*ee*	Taiwan	*Teye*-wahn
		t'ang-juk	dang-jook
In Hi	Een Hee	Tan Gun	*Tan* Goon
In Su	Een Soo	Tumen	*Too*-men
Kayakum	*Kye*-yah-kum	Ulchiro	Ool-*cheer*-oh
kimchi	keem-jee		
Kim Chun Won	Kim Joon Wahn	won	wahn
Kim Eun Kee	Kim Yoon Kee		
Kimpo	keem-poh	Yalu	*Yah*-loo
Kim Sung Kee	Kim Sung Kee	Yi Sun Sin	*Yee* Soon Seen
Kim Yun Sook	Kim Yoon Suk	Yongdongpo	Yung-dong-poh
kum-mu	*koom*-moo		
mudang-choom	moo-*dahng*-joom		

* Italics indicate accent. Where no syllables are italicized the stress is equal.

HOW TO SAY IT IN KOREAN *

English: Hello
Korean: Anyaha simnika
Pronunciation: Ahn-eeh-ah *sim*-nee-kah

English: Thank you
Korean: Kamsa hamnida
Pronunciation: *Kahm*-sah *Hahm*-nee-dah

English: Good-bye
Korean: Aniyohika sipsio (to person
leaving)
Pronunciation: *Ahn*-yung-hee-kah
sip-see-yoh
Korean: Aniyohiki sipsio (to person
staying behind)
Pronunciation: *Ahn*-yung-hee-key
sip-see-yoh

English: We are friends
Korean: Dongsin wun nawi chinku
imnida
Pronunciation: *Dahng*-sin oon *nah*-wih
chin-koo *im*-nee-dah

* Italics indicate pronunciation, where there no italics, the stress is equal.

HISTORICAL OUTLINE

2000 B.C. — Tribesmen from what is now Manchuria and Northern China come to the peninsula.

1200 B.C. —First settlement founded at Pyongyang by a Chinese scholar, Ki-tze.

A.D. 7th century — Silla kingdom, a united government, established.

1592 — Chinese and Korean forces repel a Japanese invasion. China becomes Korea's protector.

17th–19th centuries — Isolated from the rest of the world, Korea develops her own way of life.

1876–1910 — Japanese take over Korea and make it a colony.

1919 — Koreans unsuccessfully revolt against Japanese.

1945 — After Japanese defeat in World War II, Korea is divided at the 38th parallel with the Soviet Union occupying the northern section and the United States occupying the south.

1950 — North Koreans invade southern Korea, which is defended by U.N. troops.

1960 — Revolt against South Korean government is spearheaded by college students.

1961 — Army takes over the southern government.

Present — The two sections of Korea work to develop their economy, with the people hoping that foreign occupation may eventually be ended and the country reunited. This hope is a dim one for the predictable future, however.

Index

63

THE GETTING TO KNOW BOOKS
COVER TODAY'S WORLD

Africa

GETTING TO KNOW AFRICA'S FRENCH COMMUNITY
GETTING TO KNOW ALGERIA
GETTING TO KNOW EGYPT
GETTING TO KNOW KENYA
GETTING TO KNOW LIBERIA
GETTING TO KNOW NIGERIA
GETTING TO KNOW THE SAHARA
GETTING TO KNOW SOUTH AFRICA
GETTING TO KNOW SOUTHERN RHODESIA
      ZAMBIA AND MALAWI
GETTING TO KNOW TANGANYIKA

Arctic

GETTING TO KNOW THE ARCTIC

Asia

GETTING TO KNOW BURMA
GETTING TO KNOW THE CENTRAL HIMALAYAS
GETTING TO KNOW HONG KONG
GETTING TO KNOW INDIA
GETTING TO KNOW JAPAN
GETTING TO KNOW KOREA
GETTING TO KNOW MALAYA
GETTING TO KNOW THE NORTHERN HIMALAYAS
GETTING TO KNOW PAKISTAN
GETTING TO KNOW THE RIVER GANGES
GETTING TO KNOW THAILAND
GETTING TO KNOW THE TWO CHINAS
GETTING TO KNOW THE TWO KOREAS
GETTING TO KNOW THE TWO VIETNAMS

Caribbean and Central America

GETTING TO KNOW THE BRITISH WEST INDIES
GETTING TO KNOW COSTA RICA, EL SALVADOR
      AND NICARAGUA
GETTING TO KNOW CUBA
GETTING TO KNOW GUATEMALA
      AND THE TWO HONDURAS
GETTING TO KNOW MEXICO
GETTING TO KNOW PANAMA
GETTING TO KNOW PUERTO RICO
GETTING TO KNOW THE VIRGIN ISLANDS

Europe, East and West

GETTING TO KNOW FRANCE
GETTING TO KNOW GERMANY

GETTING TO KNOW GREECE
GETTING TO KNOW ITALY
GETTING TO KNOW POLAND
GETTING TO KNOW SCANDINAVIA
GETTING TO KNOW SPAIN
GETTING TO KNOW SWITZERLAND
GETTING TO KNOW THE SOVIET UNION

Middle East

GETTING TO KNOW IRAN-IRAQ
GETTING TO KNOW ISRAEL
GETTING TO KNOW LEBANON
GETTING TO KNOW SAUDI ARABIA
GETTING TO KNOW TURKEY

North America

GETTING TO KNOW ALASKA
GETTING TO KNOW AMERICAN INDIANS TODAY
GETTING TO KNOW CANADA
GETTING TO KNOW THE MISSISSIPPI RIVER
GETTING TO KNOW THE U.S.A.

Pacific

GETTING TO KNOW AUSTRALIA
GETTING TO KNOW HAWAII
GETTING TO KNOW INDONESIA
GETTING TO KNOW MALAYSIA
GETTING TO KNOW THE PHILIPPINES
GETTING TO KNOW THE SOUTH PACIFIC

South America

GETTING TO KNOW ARGENTINA
GETTING TO KNOW BRAZIL
GETTING TO KNOW CHILE
GETTING TO KNOW COLOMBIA
GETTING TO KNOW PERU
GETTING TO KNOW THE RIVER AMAZON
GETTING TO KNOW VENEZUELA

United Nations Agencies

GETTING TO KNOW F.A.O.
GETTING TO KNOW
      THE HUMAN RIGHTS COMMISSION
GETTING TO KNOW UNESCO
GETTING TO KNOW UNICEF
GETTING TO KNOW W H O
GETTING TO KNOW WMO

COWARD-McCANN, INC. · 200 MADISON AVENUE · NEW YORK 16, N. Y.